Special God

Julie Melilli

Illustrated by Matt Stevens

CROSSWAY®

WHEATON, ILLINOIS

Library of Congress Cataloging-in-Publication Data

Names: Melilli, Julie, 1973- author. | Stevens, Matthew illustrator.

Title: Special God / Julie Melilli ; illustrated by Matt Stevens.

Description: Wheaton : Crossway, 2018.

Identifiers: LCCN 2017060545 | ISBN 9781433562518 (hc)

Subjects: LCSH: Theology, Doctrinal--Juvenile literature.

Classification: LCC BT107 .M45 2018 | DDC 230--dc23

LC record available at https://lccn.loc.gov/2017060545

Crossway is a publishing ministry of Good News Publishers.

RRD		28	27	26	25	24	23	22	21	20	19	18
15	14	13	12	11	10	9	8	7	6	5	4	3	2	1

FOR JOSIE GRACE

Thankful that God added you to me
and that he continues to add his grace to us all

Contents

Introduction

A few years ago I set out to find a book that I could read with my daughter to teach her about who God is and what it means to believe in him. There were some pretty specific criteria that needed to be met for this important book. It needed to take into account her physical differences and her developmental disabilities as well as her unique background; she had spent many years in an orphanage before being adopted into our family.

My search led me to heaps of books. Some were biblically sound but referenced Bible stories or church traditions to which my daughter had never been exposed. Others were well-written but full of confusing vocabulary for a non-native English speaker. Many well-meaning books caused unintentional angst by mentioning "when you were a baby with your mom" or "how much you look like your brothers" and other experiences that my daughter couldn't relate to. Lastly, I found many books that used word pictures and figurative language to explain God. These were hindrances for my daughter whose limited vocabulary and learning difficulties made it essential for things to be simple and concrete.

Alas, I couldn't find the book I was looking for . . . so I decided to write it.

And as I've written, I've realized that we all have special needs that affect how we understand God. But, we all need to know that God is for the smart and the strong as well as the different and the disabled. He sent his Son Jesus for the distinguished and for the dysfunctional. This book is for my daughter, but it's also for anyone, indeed everyone, who has never heard or never fully understood this very special story of a very special God.

God

Who is God?

God is God.
He's very special.
There is no one like him.

He is not a person like you and me. He has always been alive and
will never die. He is **invisible** which means you can't see him.

God created and controls the world. **Created** means he made it.
Controls means he's the boss of it.

God has a home in heaven, but he can be everywhere.
He can see and hear everything. He knows and loves everybody.

Also God is perfect. **Perfect** means he never makes a mistake.
He is always good and right.

God is kind and wise. **Wise** means he is really smart, but
more than that, he uses his smartness to always make
the best right choice.

God is love. **Love** is choosing to think about what's best for someone else and then cheerfully doing it.

That's what God does.

He has chosen to put your needs above his own and to do whatever it takes to give you what you need.

God loves you very much.

"God is love." (1 John 4:8)

God Is Holy

God is God. He is not a regular person like you and me.

There are many things that are different about God and people:
    God is perfect. People are not perfect.
    God never makes a mistake. People make lots of mistakes.
    God is invisible. People are not invisible.

But the biggest difference between God and people is that God is holy and people are not.

Holy means he's the only one like him.
There is no one anywhere that can be God except for God.

He is set apart all by himself.
He isn't just better than us, he's the best.
He isn't just more than us, he's the most.
He is the best at everything.
The best maker and thinker and helper.
He is the most of everything.
The most loving and fair and right.
He is the best and the most of all things that are good and true.

That's what holy means.

God's holiness is one of the most important and special things about him. If you understand his holiness, you will understand why God does what he does. His holiness is what makes him God. There is no one like him.

"There is none holy like the LORD: for there is none besides you." (1 Samuel 2:2)

Sin

Sin is anything you

say or

do or

think

that is not what God wants you to

say or

do or

think.

God wants us to love him and others. When we don't
love him or love other people, we are sinning.

When you say unkind words, when you lie, or when you
make fun of someone—that is sin.

When you fight, when you hit or kick somebody, or when you take
something that's not yours—that is sin.

When you think only about making yourself happy and not
others, when you think about bad things you want to do,
or when you worry about stuff—that is sin.

A person who sins is called a **sinner**.
Every person in the world is a sinner.
All grown-ups and all children are sinners.
Everyone is a sinner except for God and Jesus.

God loves you, but he doesn't love your sin.
He wants you to stop sinning. You need his help to stop sinning.

When God looks at you he sees and knows everything about you.
He sees all that's wonderful about you, but he also sees all your sin.

You will never be perfect, and you will always be a sinner.
But God can help you sin less and love more.

"All have sinned and fall short of the glory of God." (Romans 3:23)

God's Holiness Is Important

God is holy.

He is set apart from everyone else.

He is the best and the most of all things that are good and true.

He has never sinned and will never sin.

He is perfect and will always be perfect.

He knows everything and can do everything.

He is the only one like him.

The most important difference between God and people is his holiness. To understand why God does what he does, you must understand his holiness.

God's holiness has great power. Because of his powerful holiness, he cannot be around anyone or anything that is not holy. His holiness sets him apart from you.

But God wants to be with you! He loves you!

God knows you're not holy; he can see your sin. **Sin** is when you say or do or think anything that God doesn't want you to say or do or think. All people, even really nice people, are sinful. Sin makes you un-holy.

You can be near God if
you become holy like him.
If you never sin, you can be with
holy God. Can you make sure you never
sin again? Of course not! That is impossible.
Impossible means it can never ever happen.

God can only be with you if you have no sin. You can't get rid
of your own sin; that is impossible. Someone has to take your
sin away from you. You can't do it yourself.

Holy God loves un-holy you. He wants to be with un-holy you
so much that he has made a way for your sins to be taken away.
He has a very special plan. What is impossible for you to do is
possible for God to do.

Sin Brings Separation

Sin is anything you say or do or think that is not what God wants you to say or do or think.

God doesn't sin. He is holy. When you sin you are separated from God. **Separated** means you are kept away from God.

God knows you are not holy; he sees your sin. His holiness separates him from you and your sin separates you from him.

God loves you and wants to have a good relationship with you. A **good relationship** is when you like someone, and they like you, and you enjoy spending time together.

When you have a good relationship with someone, you want to make that person happy.

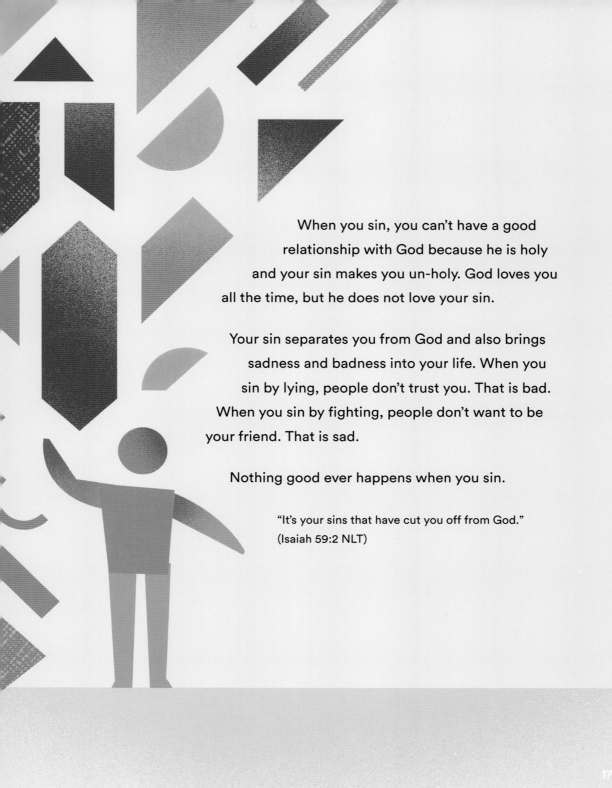

When you sin, you can't have a good relationship with God because he is holy and your sin makes you un-holy. God loves you all the time, but he does not love your sin.

Your sin separates you from God and also brings sadness and badness into your life. When you sin by lying, people don't trust you. That is bad. When you sin by fighting, people don't want to be your friend. That is sad.

Nothing good ever happens when you sin.

"It's your sins that have cut you off from God."
(Isaiah 59:2 NLT)

Prayer and Confession

Sin is anything you say or do or think that is not what God wants you to say or do or think.

When you sin, you are separated from God. You can't have a good relationship with him when you sin.

If you want to have a good relationship with him, here's what you need to do: After you sin, you need to tell God that you sinned and tell him you are sorry for sinning.

That is called confession.

Confession is telling God that you have sinned and saying you're sorry for sinning.

The way you tell God is by praying. **Praying** means talking to God.

Even though you can't see God, he can hear you when you pray. You can pray anytime and anywhere. Sometimes you can pray without talking. You can just think the words you want to say to God. He knows what you are praying even when you don't say words out loud.

Confession means telling God that you know you are a sinner and that you are sorry for your sins.

God wants to have a good relationship with you, but that can only happen when you confess your sins.

"But I confess my sins; I am deeply sorry for what I have done." (Psalm 38:18 NLT)

Forgiveness

God loves you very much, but he hates it when you sin.

He is loving, but he is also holy. God knows you sin; he sees your sin. When you sin, you can't have a good relationship with him; you are separated from him. The only way to be back together with God after you sin is to confess your sin.

Confess means to tell God that you sinned and that you're sorry for your sin. Pray to God and tell him what you did. Tell him you are sorry and don't want to do it again. When you do that, God forgives you.

Forgives means God hears your prayer that says "I am sorry for my sin," and he tells you, "I know you sinned, and I love you still."

When God forgives you, he looks at you and sees all the wonderful things about you and no longer sees your sin. It's amazing!

God forgives you when you confess. He sees you, but not your sin. You aren't separated from him anymore. He still loves you.

When you confess your sins, God forgives you, and you have a good relationship with him again.

"If we confess our sins, he is faithful and just to forgive us our sins." (1 John 1:9)

Special God

When you **confess** your sins to God, when you tell him you're sorry for your sins, he forgives you.

He hears you pray, and he tells you that he still loves you. That's **forgiveness**. When he forgives you, he no longer sees your sin; it's all gone!

God is the only person who can forgive your sins. Nobody else can forgive your sins.

Some people think that if they try really hard to be good, they will never sin again, but that's not true. People will always sin. Even though you want to stop sinning, you will always sin and never be able to fully stop. You will need to keep confessing your sins to God, and he will keep forgiving you.

Every time you sin, God will know. When he looks at you, he will see all the wonderful things about you, but he will also see your sin.

God knows you are a sinner, but he loves you anyway and wants to have a good relationship with you.

Because it's impossible to stop sinning, at the end of your life your sins will separate you from God forever.

God doesn't want that! He doesn't want you to be separated from him forever. He wants to have a good relationship with you now and after you die too!

He's a special, special God! And he has a very special plan for how to have a good relationship with you now and after you die. He has a plan to take away your sins. It's called "God's plan of salvation."

"If we confess our sins, he is faithful and just to forgive us our sins." (1 John 1:9)

Salvation

When you sin you are separated from God. You must confess your sins to God and he will forgive you. When he forgives you, he doesn't see your sin anymore!

Because no one can stop sinning, at the end of your life you will have sin that will keep you separated from God forever. God loves you and doesn't want that to happen.

So God has made a plan of salvation.

Salvation means to be saved.

Saved means to be helped so that you don't get hurt or die.

If you run out in the street when a car is coming, you need someone to get you out of the way so that you don't get hurt or die. You need to be saved from the car.

If you fall into a lake, and you can't swim, you need someone to pull you out so that you don't get hurt or die. You need to be saved from the lake.

You can't save yourself. Someone else has to save you.

When you sin, you are putting yourself in a dangerous place by separating yourself from God. A dangerous place is any place where you could get hurt. Being separated from God would hurt very much.

You need someone to save you so that you can have a good relationship with God forever. There's only one person who can save you, and that person is God.

Salvation means being saved from your sins forever by God.

"Everyone who calls on the name of the LORD will be saved." (Joel 2:32 NIV)

Consequences

Before you understand God's plan of salvation,
you need to know about consequences.

A **consequence** is what happens after you do something.
Consequences can be good or bad.

For example, after you clean up your room, you feel proud.
That is a good consequence. After you eat a whole bunch of
candy, you feel sick. That is a bad consequence.

After you are kind to someone, you have a new friend. That is a
good consequence. After you lie to someone, you lose a friend.
That is a bad consequence.

Sin only has bad consequences. The worst consequence
of sin is separation from God.

Because everyone sins, everyone has bad consequences.
We all need to be saved from those consequences.

God is the only one who can save us.

He has made a way so that you don't have to be
separated from him forever.

God uses his Son, Jesus, to save you from the consequences of
sin. Jesus is the most important part of God's plan of salvation.

"For God did not send his Son into the world to condemn the world, but in order
that the world might be saved through him." (John 3:17)

Condemn means to say that something is totally bad and
that you don't like it at all.

Jesus

Who is Jesus?

Jesus is God's only Son.

Jesus lived on earth for about thirty-three years. Just like you,
Jesus started as a baby, and then he was a kid, and a teenager,
and finally an adult. He did regular stuff that all people do.
He could read and write and walk and talk. Jesus had friends
and a family. He got hungry and tired and sad and mad.

But Jesus is very special.
He was a regular person except for one thing: he never sinned.
Jesus never did anything wrong.
He never lied or disobeyed, and he was never mean.
Just like God, he is perfect.
And just like God, he is holy.

The reason that Jesus lived on earth for a while was because he was the most important part of God's amazing plan of salvation and God's plan would be taking place on earth. Only because of Jesus are you able to have a good relationship with God. Jesus is the reason that you can be with holy God.

Jesus is the person God used to get rid of the consequence of sin. Because of Jesus, you can stop being separated from God when you sin.

"You [Jesus] are the Christ, the Son of the living God." (Matthew 16:16)

Punishments

When you sin, there is a consequence.

A **consequence** is what happens after you do something. A consequence can be good or bad.

The consequence of sin is always bad: separation from God.

After a bad consequence, there is often a punishment.

A **punishment** is something that happens to you to help you understand that what you did was wrong. A punishment can also be a way for you to try to make things better.

For example, if you take something that isn't yours, the consequence is that people won't trust you, and the punishment may be that you have to pay money for what you took.

When you sin, you must confess your sin, and God will forgive you. But there may still be a punishment as part of the consequence of your sin.

When you sin, the consequence is that you are separated from God, and the punishment for sin is death.

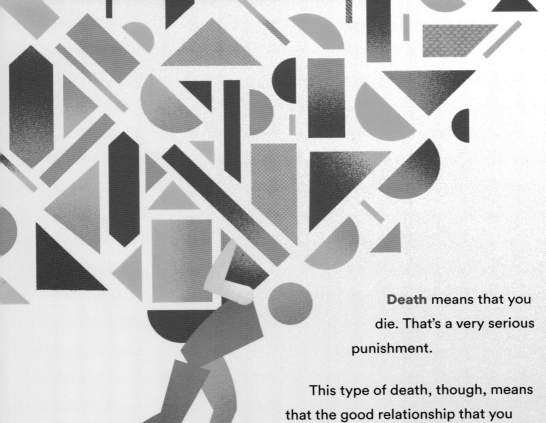

Death means that you die. That's a very serious punishment.

This type of death, though, means that the good relationship that you have with God will die. You will not die every time you sin.

God loves you and wants to have a happy, living relationship with you. He doesn't want your good relationship to die. But when you sin it is impossible for holy God to be with you. When you sin, your happy, living relationship turns into a sad, dead relationship.

God loves you so much that he made a way for someone else to take your punishment. Your relationship with God doesn't have to die even when you sin! He has made another way for the wrong to be made right! He is an amazing God!

Jesus Instead of You

Your sin brings consequences and consequences bring punishment. God wants to save you from the punishment that comes from your sins.

When you sin, the consequence is that you are separated from God and the punishment for sin is death.

God doesn't want any person to die because of their sins. But somebody has to take the punishment so that things can be made right again.

God has made a special plan to take the punishment of your sins away from you.

God's plan happened a long time ago; long before you were born. Even though you weren't born yet, God knew all about you. He knew the wonderful stuff but he also knew the sin stuff.

So here's God's plan: Instead of God seeing your sin on you, he is going to see it on Jesus. Instead of you getting blamed for your sin, Jesus will get blamed.

Blamed means saying that someone did something wrong.

Jesus, who never sinned, will get blamed for all your sin. When God looks at Jesus, he will see your sin. But it won't be yours anymore, it will be Jesus's. Because of that sin, Jesus will be separated from God instead of you. Jesus will have the consequence and punishment instead of you.

Jesus won't be separated from God forever, and he won't be punished forever. But when he takes your punishment, things will be made right forever.

You should be the one with the punishment because you are the one who sinned. But God chose Jesus, his only Son, to take your sin and punishment instead.

This is God's plan to save you.

"You know that he [Jesus] appeared [came] in order to take away sins, and in him there is no sin." (1 John 3:5)

Jesus Was Crucified

God loves you so much. He doesn't want you to be separated from him when you sin.

God has made a special plan to take the punishment of your sins away from you.

Instead of God seeing your sin on you, he is going to see it on Jesus. Instead of you getting blamed for your sin, Jesus will get blamed. God chose Jesus, his only Son, to be blamed for your sin and take your punishment.

Even though Jesus never sinned, God chose to see your sin on Jesus. And because Jesus had your sin on him, he also had your punishment on him and that punishment was death.

Long, long ago, at the end of the time that Jesus lived on earth, he was crucified. **Crucified** means to be killed by being nailed to a wooden cross. It is a horrible, horrible thing. In Bible times, some people would be crucified as punishment if they had done something very bad.

But Jesus had never done anything bad! He had never done anything wrong! He was crucified even though he was not a sinner. Because, through God's plan, Jesus was covered with everyone's sin, Jesus got the punishment that all of us should have had.

Jesus, who never sinned, became sin for you and took your punishment willingly. **Willingly** means he chose to do it. No one had to make him do it.

Jesus was crucified; he died on a cross, so that you wouldn't have to die for your sins. He died so that your good relationship with God could stay alive. How amazing!

"He [God] made him [Jesus] to be sin who knew no sin." (2 Corinthians 5:21)

Jesus Was Resurrected

Jesus took on himself all the sins you have ever done or ever will do. He was punished for the sins of all the people in all the world. At the end of his life here on earth, Jesus was crucified. He died on a cross.

It was very sad. Jesus was dead.

He died on the cross and was buried in a tomb. A **tomb** is a place where a dead body is put.

The first three days after Jesus died were terrible. All of his family and friends were so sad. They cried and tried to help each other feel better, but they were just sad, sad, sad.

But at the end of those three days, there was a miracle. A **miracle** is an amazing surprise that only God can make happen.

The miracle was that Jesus, who was dead, came back to life! He was dead, and then he wasn't! He was alive!

This is known as the resurrection of Jesus. **Resurrection** means rising from the dead and coming back to life.

Jesus left the tomb and went to visit his family and friends who were so sad. When they saw him, they couldn't believe it! Standing right in front of them was Jesus! The same person who had been crucified three days before was alive again! What a miracle!

Their sadness changed into joy. **Joy** is a feeling of great happiness. Instead of sad, sad, sad now there was joy, joy, joy!

Jesus came back to life a long, long time ago, and he is still alive today. He isn't living on earth anymore, so you won't see him walking around. But, he is alive today, still perfect and sinless, and lives in heaven with God. **Heaven** is God's home.

"He is not here, but has risen." (Luke 24:6)

Jesus Is Really God's Son

Jesus took the sin of all people and was crucified as a punishment.
He died on the cross because of everyone's sin.

Jesus had to die because God can't be around sinful people.
God is loving, but he is holy.

Someone has to be punished for sin.
God chose Jesus to be the one who was punished.
Jesus went willingly to die on the cross.

Jesus died on the cross for everybody's sin, but after three days,
he was resurrected. He came back to life! It was a miracle!

A **miracle** is an amazing surprise that only God can do.

God is full of miracles. One of his miracles is that he brought
Jesus back to life at the resurrection.

Another one of God's miracles is that now he sees you as holy
because of Jesus. He sees you as having no sin. It's a miracle!

Jesus took all the sin that you had, and he gave you all the holiness that he has. Now when God sees you, he doesn't see your sin, because Jesus took it to the cross. God sees you as holy because Jesus gave you his holiness when he took your sins to the cross.

The resurrection is important.

One reason it's important is because it proves that Jesus is really God's Son.

Proves means it shows that it's true.

A regular person couldn't come back to life and then stay alive forever like Jesus has. Only someone who is God or has all of God's power can come back to life and stay alive. Jesus is God's Son and has all the same power that God has. That's why he could come back to life.

"Jesus Christ our Lord . . . by being raised from the dead . . . was proved to be the mighty Son of God." (Romans 1:3–4 TLB)

God Can Really Forgive Sin

When Jesus came back to life at the resurrection, it was more than just a miracle, it was the only way that you can have a good relationship with God forever.

The resurrection is important for many reasons. First of all, when Jesus came back to life he proved that he was truly God's Son. Only someone with God's power could come back to life and stay alive like Jesus has.

Second, it proves that God has the power to forgive our sin. **Proves** means it shows that it's true. God can truly forgive our sins.

Jesus had no sin. But he took your sin and died with it on the cross. Then he was resurrected.

God brought Jesus back to life, but the punishment of death stayed dead. If God can do that, he can also forgive sins.

The punishment that Jesus took for your sin made the wrong thing right. Because Jesus took your punishment, you can live in a good relationship with God again.

Jesus was punished for your sin when he died on the cross, but that doesn't mean that you will never sin again. You are a person, so you will always sin. But now when you sin, you know that you can confess and be forgiven and keep on having a good relationship with God.

Even though you will keep sinning over and over again, Jesus only had to die once on the cross. He is so powerful that he only had to die one time for you to be forgiven for all of your sins forever.

"If Christ has not been raised . . . you are still in your sins." (1 Corinthians 15:17)

Jesus Defeated Death

When God did a miracle and raised Jesus from the dead, which is called the resurrection, he did it for some very important reasons.

First, Jesus's resurrection proves he is the Son of God. It shows you that it's true.

Second, his resurrection proves that God can forgive sins. Jesus took your punishment for sin, and he gave you his holiness so that you can be forgiven by God.

Another reason the resurrection is important is it proves that Jesus is more powerful than death.

When someone dies they are dead forever; they will never be alive again. Their body will never move or think or eat or see anything. They are dead. Death is very strong.

But Jesus died and then came back to life, which proves that he is stronger than death. He defeated death. **Defeat** means to beat and win. He beat death. Jesus won, death lost.

You have a body that will someday die, but because Jesus defeated death when he died on the cross and rose again, you can beat death if you follow him.

Someday your body will die, but an even more important part of you will not. God has a wonderful plan to save you while you're alive and also when you die.

"We are sure of this because Christ was raised from the dead, and he will never die again. Death no longer has any power over him." (Romans 6:9 NLT)

Physical and Spiritual Body

Someday your body will die, but an even more important part of you will not. That part is called your **spirit**, or your **soul**.

Everyone has a body. It is the part of you that you can see and touch. You can see your legs. You can touch your skin. You can see your fingers and feel your hair. Your body can get sick and dirty. It needs to be cleaned and fed and taken care of. Your body is also called your **physical self**.

Your physical self is important. You need it to be able to live on earth. You need your eyes to see, and your brain to think, and your feet to move you around.

Everybody also has a spirit. It is the part of you that you can't see or touch. Your spirit makes you different than every other person. Your physical self may look like someone else, but your spirit, or your spiritual self, is like nobody else.

Your spirit controls the way you think and feel about things. It's the part of you that wants to be nice sometimes and mean sometimes. Your spirit controls the things you like and the things you hate. It also controls how you treat other people. Your spirit can feel joyful, or tired, or excited, or worried.

Your spirit is the part of you that knows about God and decides whether or not to have a relationship with him. Your spirit is the part of you that feels bad when you sin and feels happy when you are forgiven. Your spirit is the part of you that knows that God is with you even though you can't see him or hear him.

God has given you these two different parts, your physical self and your spiritual self, for a very special reason.

Mystery

This story of how God made a way for us to have a good relationship with him can be kind of confusing. **Confusing** means hard to understand. Learning that you have two parts, physical and spiritual, may also be confusing.

The **Bible** tells us that many things about God and Jesus are simple enough for a child to understand. **Simple** means easy.

But it also tells us that God is so much wiser than all of us that he does many things that we will never understand no matter how smart or old we are. Even the smartest and oldest people in the world don't totally understand everything about God.

Many of the things that God does and the way he works in the world are a mystery to us. A **mystery** is something that is difficult or impossible to explain. **Impossible** means it can't be done. For those things that are a mystery, we should learn as much as we can from people who do understand it, and then trust God for the rest. **Trust** means we believe that what God says in the Bible is true, and we believe even when we don't understand everything about it.

God knows everything better than we do, and he loves us and always does the right thing. Even when we don't understand all the mysteries, we can trust in God.

You can be sure that God will help you understand anything you need to know that's important. He says in the Bible that he will give understanding to anyone who asks for it. You can pray and ask him for help if you need to. You can also ask someone else who knows God to help you understand.

"If you need wisdom, ask . . . God, and he will give it to you." (James 1:5 NLT)

Eternal Life

Your body has two parts:

Your **physical self** that you can see and touch.

And your **spiritual self**, which is your spirit or soul,
that you can't see or touch but which makes you who
you are and connects you to God.

Your physical self will die someday. Everyone on earth will die.
Nobody knows when that will happen, but we know it will.

When a person dies, his or her body goes into a tomb, also called a
grave, just like Jesus. But, unlike Jesus, when a body dies, it does not
come back to life. When you die, your physical self is dead.

But remember you are more than just your body, your physical self. You also have a spiritual self.

Your spiritual self, which you can't see or touch, doesn't die. Your spirit, or soul, doesn't go in to the grave with your body.

Here is what happens to your spiritual self:
When you die, if you believed in Jesus, and that he died because of your sins, your spiritual self will keep living forever. Your spiritual self will have eternal life.

Eternal life means to live forever and ever and ever and never die.

Not only will your spirit live forever, it will live forever in a good relationship with God.

Because Jesus took the punishment for your sin on the cross, God now looks at your spiritual self and sees it as sinless, like Jesus.

When Jesus took your punishment, things were made right. Now you are able to be with holy God forever.

Your spiritual self will have eternal life with God and Jesus in heaven. Your body will stay dead, but your spirit will live forever.

"For God so loved the world, that he gave his only Son, that whoever believes in him should not perish [die] but have eternal life." (John 3:16)

Heaven

When your physical self dies, your spiritual self can have eternal life in heaven with God. You can have a good relationship with him forever because of what Jesus did when he took your punishment on the cross.

Heaven is one more of the mysteries of God. It is something that is difficult or impossible to explain.

God has created heaven as a wonderful place to live with him after you die. God's plan is for your spiritual self to live with him in heaven after your physical self dies on earth.

A lot about heaven is a mystery, but the Bible tells us a little bit about it. It tells us that heaven is an amazing place. In heaven, everything is beautiful and full of life. There will be no more sin or sickness. People will all get along with each other, and everyone will be friends. But the very best thing about heaven is that you can be with God forever.

It's not a place you can get to on an airplane or in a car. God uses his miracle powers to get you to heaven. Your physical self doesn't go there, so you don't need to take anything. You can only go there if you die, and your spiritual self believes in God.

You don't need to understand everything about heaven for you to believe it is true. You can trust God. He is wiser than you, and he loves you. He will take care of you on earth and in heaven.

Grace and Faith

God and Jesus did everything for you to be saved.

God sent Jesus to earth to take your punishment. Jesus took your sin and your punishment when he died on the cross. God raised Jesus from the dead. Jesus now lives forever with God in heaven.

God loves you so much that he did all this for you. He wants to save you and give you eternal life. He wants to have a good relationship with you now and in heaven.

You don't have to do anything for him to save you.
You don't have to do anything for him to give you eternal life.

He is giving you all of this as a free gift. You didn't do anything to get it, and you don't deserve it. **Deserve** it means you're supposed to get it because of something you've done. But you didn't do anything to get all this. You don't deserve it. God just loves you and wants to be with you.

He gave you these wonderful gifts—salvation and eternal life—that you don't deserve. That is called grace. **Grace** means undeserved gifts.

There is one thing you have to do when God gives you a gift: you have to take it by faith. **Faith** means believing all the things about God, even those things that are mysteries. God gives you the gift of salvation when you believe that he sent his Son Jesus to die on the cross for your sins, and you believe that Jesus was raised from the dead.

All the good things that God does for you and the good gifts he gives you are all grace. And they are all yours if you have faith in him.

"For by grace you have been saved through faith. And this is not your own doing; it is the gift of God." (Ephesians 2:8)

Becoming a Christian

Now that you know about God's plan of salvation, you have a choice to make:

You can choose to believe that it's all true and accept God's gift of salvation by faith, or you can choose to believe it's not true and choose to not accept it. **Accept** means take it.

A person who chooses to believe that Jesus is God's Son, that he took the punishment for all our sins, and that he was raised from the dead to make a way for us to have a good relationship with God is called a **Christian**.

If you are a Christian, it means you are a person who believes in and follows Christ. **Christ** is another name for Jesus.

Do you believe Jesus is God's Son?
Do you believe Jesus died on the cross as punishment for your sins?
Do you believe he was resurrected?
Do you want to confess your sins and be forgiven?
Do you want to have a good relationship with God?

If your answer is "yes," then you are ready to become a Christian.

To accept God's gift, you pray.
Tell God that you believe Jesus is his Son, and that Jesus died for your sins.
Confess your sins to God and ask him to forgive you.
Tell him that you love him, and that you want to have a good relationship with him.
Ask him to fill your heart with love for him.
Ask him to fill your mind with thoughts of him.
Ask him to fill your life with ways to show other people how wonderful he is.

When you do that, you are a Christian.

"If you confess with your mouth that Jesus is Lord and believe in your heart that God raised him from the dead, you will be saved." (Romans 10:9)

Following Jesus

A Christian is a person who believes in God and wants to follow Jesus. Following Jesus means learning about how Jesus lived on earth and trying to live the same way.

Jesus was patient and kind and helpful. He was loving and gentle and truthful. A Christian will want to be the same.

One thing that Christians do is read the Bible.
The **Bible** is God's written book. It tells you everything you need to know about God and how to follow Jesus.

If you are a Christian, you will want to go to church.
The **church** is God's family on earth. God's family is made up of everyone who is a Christian. Christians go to church to have friends who also believe in God and can help them understand how to follow Jesus.

Also Christians pray. **Praying** is talking to God.
The Bible tells us that God wants you to talk to him about everything.
He wants you to talk to him when you're happy and when you're sad.
You can talk to him to tell him "thank you" and to ask him for help.

Reading the Bible, going to church, and praying are not things you
have to do to become a Christian; they are things that you will want
to do when you are a Christian.

A Christian is still a regular person.
A Christian still sins.
A Christian still has to confess and be forgiven.
But Christians know that even when they sin, they are loved by God.

Nothing can change what Jesus did for you on the cross.
If you believe in God and if you follow Jesus, you are a Christian forever.

Being a Christian means that for the rest of your life, on earth and in
heaven, your special needs will be cared for by a special God.

"From his fullness we have all received, grace upon grace." (John 1:16)

Words to Know

accept: to take

Bible: a book that is God's Word

blame: to say that someone did something wrong

Christ: another name for Jesus

Christian: a Christ-follower

church: God's family on earth

condemn: to say something is totally bad and that you don't like it at all

confess/confession: telling God that you sinned and that you're sorry for your sin

confusing: hard to understand

consequence: what happens after you do something

control: to be the boss of

created: made

crucified: to be killed by being nailed to a wooden cross

death: another word for when you die

defeat: to beat and win

deserve: to get something as a result of something you've done

eternal life: to live forever and ever and ever and never die

faith: believing without understanding everything or being able to see it

forgive/forgiveness: when God hears your confession and tells you, "I know you sinned, and I love you still."

God: the Creator and ruler of the world

good relationship: when you like someone, and they like you, and you enjoy being together

grace: undeserved gifts; specifically, salvation and eternal life

heaven: God's home

holy/holiness: set apart, perfect, always right, always good, the best

impossible: it can never happen

invisible: can't be seen

Jesus: God's Son

joy: a feeling of great happiness

love: choosing to think about what's best for someone else and cheerfully doing it

miracle: an amazing surprise that only God can do

mystery: something that is difficult or impossible to explain

perfect: never mistaken or wrong

physical self: your body; the part of you that can be seen and touched

praying: talking to God

prove: to show something is true

punishment: something that happens to you to help you understand that what you did was wrong. It can also be a way to try to make things better.

resurrection: rising from the dead and coming back to life

salvation: to be saved from your sins forever by God

saved: to be helped so that you don't get hurt or die

separated: kept away from; apart

simple: easy

sin: anything you say or do or think that is not what God wants you to say or do or think

sinner: a person who sins

spirit/soul: the part of you that makes up your spiritual self. It is the part you can't see or touch, but it makes you who you are. It is your feelings and thoughts and likes.

tomb: a place where a dead body is put

trust: believing that something or someone is truthful

willingly: to choose to do something

wise: really smart and able to always make the right choice